Crystals

The Complete Crystal Healing Guide

Heal the Body, Mind, and Soul with these Amazing Crystals

Table of Contents:

Introduction 3

Chapter 1 - Crystal Healing 7

Chapter 2 - The Seven Chakras 10

Chapter 3 - Healing Crystals and their Uses 15

Chapter 4 - Clearing Crystals 27

Chapter 5 - Dedicating and Programming Crystals . 29

Chapter 6 - How to Use Crystals 31

Conclusion 35

Introduction

Thank you and congratulations for downloading the book, *"Crystals: The Complete Crystal Healing Guide (Heal the Body, Mind, and Soul with these Amazing Crystals)"*.

Do you always find yourself feeling tired and depressed? Do you always suffer from migraines and headaches? Are you suffering from physical problems such as a nervous breakdown and diabetes? Do you need to attract good luck, love and wealth? Do you need a boost in your confidence, courage and self-worth? Do you need mind clarity and spiritual guidance? Do you need protection against outside forces or do you just want to know all about crystal healing?

Well, this book might be just for you!

This book will help you overcome not only physical ailments but also emotional ones. This will also teach you the basics about crystal healing.

This was written in order to share and spread the many benefits of crystal healing. This contains vital information regarding crystal healing, how it works, how it can be used, and the beneficial effects of the crystals. The different types of crystals were enumerated here in order to help you in selecting the right crystal for your ailments as well as your needs. Steps on clearing, programming, and dedicating crystals are also included here.

© Copyright 2015 by Emily MacLeod - All rights reserved.

This document is geared towards providing exact and reliable information in regards to the topic and issue covered. The publication is sold with the idea that the publisher is not required to render accounting, officially permitted, or otherwise, qualified services. If advice is necessary, legal or professional, a practiced individual in the profession should be ordered.

- From a Declaration of Principles which was accepted and approved equally by a Committee of the American Bar Association and a Committee of Publishers and Associations.

In no way is it legal to reproduce, duplicate, or transmit any part of this document in either electronic means or in printed format. Recording of this publication is strictly prohibited and any storage of this document is not allowed unless with written permission from the publisher. All rights reserved.

The information provided herein is stated to be truthful and consistent, in that any liability, in terms of inattention or otherwise, by any usage or abuse of any policies, processes, or directions contained within is the solitary and utter responsibility of the recipient reader. Under no circumstances will any legal responsibility or blame be held against the publisher for any reparation, damages, or monetary loss due to the information herein, either directly or indirectly.

Respective authors own all copyrights not held by the publisher.

The information herein is offered for informational purposes solely, and is universal as so. The presentation of the information is without contract or any type of guarantee assurance.

The trademarks that are used are without any consent, and the publication of the trademark is without permission or backing by the trademark owner. All trademarks and brands within this book are for clarifying purposes only and are the owned by the owners themselves, not affiliated with this document.

Chapter 1 - Crystal Healing

Crystal healing is a practice that makes use of crystals and stones to remedy emotional, psychological, and physical ailments and illnesses. Its proponents are convinced that gemstones and crystals have healing properties. Crystal healing allegedly dates back to the time of Mesopotamia. It is believed that the ancient Egyptians are among the first people to use crystals in their pyramids to attract light and to deflect negative energy and diseases.

However, its philosophy is according to Asian cultures, specifically the Chinese idea of life energy and the Hindu idea of chakras. Chakras are fountains of life energy and they connect the supernatural and physical elements of the body.

Crystal healing can be done in two ways. One way is that a healer positions the crystals, also known as "chakras", on various parts of the patient's body. Another method is the positioning of the crystals around the body in order to create an "energy grid". This is believed to envelop the patient with healing energy.

Chakra originated from a Sanskrit word meaning "wheel". As observed by the psychics, a chakra looks like a wheel containing energy that is continuously rotating. Clairvoyants, on the other hand, see chakras as colorful flowers or wheels. Chakras start at the lowest part of the spine and end at the top of the head. Although they are fixed in the spine, they are positioned on both back and front of the body.

Each chakra rotates and vibrates at different rates. The first chakra moves at the slowest rate while the seventh chakra is the fastest. Stimulation of chakra is done by using its complimentary and/or own color. The colors of the rainbow are the colors of chakra, namely red, orange, yellow, green, blue, indigo, and violet. The brightness and size of the wheels are different that depend on physical condition, energy levels, individual development, stress, or disease.

Constant equilibrium between chakras boosts a sense of well-being and health. If chakras are wide open, an individual may suffer from short circuiting because of too much energy flowing into the body. If the chakras are shut, it may lead to diseases because the energy is not flowing through.

When the chakras are in disequilibrium, or when there is blockage in energy, slowing down of the basic life force is observed. The person may feel tired, listless, depressed or out of sorts. The physical functions of the body and thought processes may be affected; hence, diseases and a negative attitude may manifest.

Most people react to bad experiences by blocking feelings; thus, putting a great deal of energy flow to a halt. This influences the development and maturation of chakras. When an individual blocks an experience, he is blocking his chakras; therefore, causing damage to them. When functioning normally, each chakra will spin clockwise, metabolizing the energies required from the energy field.

As mentioned earlier, any disequilibrium that exists within a chakra may have strong effects on our physical and emotional states. Quartz crystals can be used to re-equilibrate chakra centers and once they are balanced, the body will be restored.

Crystals are amazing tools for healing because of the piezoelectric effect. They react to the electricity that flows through the body. If sluggish energy is present, the electrical vibrations of the crystals will balance, harmonize, and stimulate energies.

Crystals are believed to be capable of alleviating stress, curing diseases, boosting creativity, enhancing psychic powers e.g. dowsing and divination, and raising levels of consciousness. It is believed that semi-precious stones have power that is unknown to science. Even though crystal healing is not popular with doctors, it remains popular at spas and in New Age health clinics. Using crystals in spas and massage clinics are said to induce relaxation.

Chapter 2 - The Seven Chakras

First Chakra (Root)

Chakras start with the root chakra, also known as Muladhara in Saskrit. The spine base at the pubic bone (front) and at the tailbone (back) is where the root chakra is located. This chakra is related to the survival needs, safety and security. It is connected to human's contact with Mother Earth, which provides man with the ability to stay grounded on the earth's plane. It also gives the energy to succeed in the business and material world.

If blocked, a person may feel anxiety, fear, insecurity and frustration. Problems such as anorexia, knee ailments and obesity may also occur. Body parts related to the root chakra are the legs, hips, sexual organs and lower back. The colors brown, red, and black and the crystals smoky quartz, garnet, and obsidian are used for this chakra.

Second Chakra (Belly)

The second chakra is the belly. Two inches under the navel is where the second chakra is located and it is held into the spine. It is related to the fundamental needs for creativity, sexuality, self-worth and intuition. It is affected by how feelings were repressed or expressed during childhood.

Equilibrium in this chakra equates to the free flow of emotions and reaching out to others sexually. When blockage of this chakra occurs, an individual may feel emotional explosions, obsessed with sex, lack energy or become manipulative. Problems such as kidney illness, stiffening of the lower back, muscle spasms and constipation may occur. The color orange and gemstones carnelian agate, orange calcite and tiger's eye are employed in this chakra.

Third Chakra (Solar Plexus)

The solar plexus is the third chakra. Its location is two inches under the breast bone in the middle behind the stomach. It is related to ego, passions, anger, impulses, strength and personal power. It is also connected with astral travel and influences, psychic development and spirit guides.

When this chakra is in equilibrium, a cheerful outlook is experienced. Self-respect, strong personal power and an outgoing attitude are felt. When in disequilibrium, an individual may suffer from emotional problems e.g. insecurity, confusion, and depression, and physical problems e.g. liver problems, digestive difficulties, diabetes, food allergies, and nervous exhaustion. The stomach, gall bladder, small intestine, pancreas and liver are the body parts included in this chakra. The color yellow and the gemstones citrine, topaz and yellow calcite are employed in this chakra.

Fourth Chakra (Heart)

The fourth chakra is the heart. Its location is behind the breastbone (front) and on the spine between the shoulder blades (back). It is related to love, spirituality and compassion. It guides an individual's ability to love. It also connects the mind and body with spirit. Heart hurts result from aura obstructions also referred to as heart scars. Upon the release of the scars, old pain are raised. However, it frees the heart for new growth.

When this chakra is in equilibrium, compassion, empathy, and friendliness are felt. When in disequilibrium, one may suffer from emotional problems such as paranoia, indecisiveness, and feeling unworthy of love and physical problems such as high blood pressure, heart attack, insomnia, and difficulty in breathing. The lungs, heart, upper back, shoulders, and circulatory system are the body parts included in this chakra. The colors pink and green and the gemstones watermelon tourmaline, kunzite, and rose quartz are employed in this chakra.

Fifth Chakra (Throat)

The fifth chakra is the throat. Its location is in the V of the collarbone. It is related to expression of creativity, sound and communication. This is where anger is usually kept and let go. When this chakra is in equilibrium, musical and artistic inspiration, balance, and good speech delivery are observed. When in disequilibrium, a person may suffer from emotional ailments e.g. holding back, feeling timid and weak, and the inability to express thought and physical ailments e.g. skin irritations, hyperthyroidism, ear infections, back pain, and sore throat. The body parts neck, throat, teeth, thyroid glands and ears are included in this chakra. The color light blue and gemstones aquamarine and azurite are mainly used in this chakra.

Sixth Chakra (Third Eye)

The sixth chakra is the third eye. Its location is over the eyes on the middle of the forehead. It is related to higher intuition, psychic ability and the light and spirit energies. It helps in eliminating selfish attitudes and purifying negative tendencies. Through this chakra, channeling and tuning into your higher self is possible.

When this chakra is in equilibrium, the fear of death and attachment to material things is absent. Telepathy, past lives, and astral travel may be experienced. When in disequilibrium, one may suffer from emotional ailments such as fear of success, egotism, and unassertiveness; and physical ailments such as blurred vision, headaches, eye strain and blindness. The brain, eyes, endocrine and lymphatic system and face are the body parts included in this chakra. The colors dark blue and purple and gemstones amethyst, lapis lazuli and sodalite are employed in this chakra.

Seventh Chakra (The Crown)

The seventh chakra is called the crown. Its location is behind the top of the skull. It is related to spirituality, dynamic thought, energy and enlightenment. It permits the flow of wisdom inwardly and it gives cosmic consciousness. It allows connection with the God/Goddess. A silver cord joins aura bodies and stretches to the crown. At birth, the soul goes through the crown and leaves through it at death.

When this chakra is in equilibrium, opening up to the Divine and accessing the subconscious and unconscious are possible. When in disequilibrium, one may suffer from emotional ailments such as frustration, destructive feelings, and sadness and physical ailments such as headaches, migraine, and depression. The colors purple and white and the gemstones Oregon opal, clear quartz crystal, and amethyst are used in this chakra.

Chapter 3 - Healing Crystals and their Uses

Crystals are essentially minerals that are formed below the surface of the Earth by virtue of repeating patterns of atoms. Each crystal has its own attributes, depending on its growth conditions and its type. The following are examples of healing crystals that are most commonly used.

Abalone: Abalone is a seashell. It holds great soothing and healing energy, which encourages a calm behavior. It has pastel rainbow colors that boost feelings of beauty, peace, love and compassion. North Americans think that it is a sacred shell and they use it with sage to deliver messages to the heavens. It is useful to wear if you need relationship guidance.

Agate: Agate is an ancient healing stone. It is referred to as a stone of strength and was used by ancient people to help in leading them to victory during wars. Agates are protective stones; thus, they are perfect to be made into medicine bags and amulets. Emotional strength, courage and self-confidence are also brought by this stone to the owner. Some types of agates are agate eyes, Botswana agate, crab fire agate, crazy lace agate, fire agate, flame agate, moss agate, and tree agate.

Amethyst: Amethyst relieves stress naturally; thus, encouraging inner strength and bringing a strong business sense and wealth to the owner. It is used for protection and spiritual growth. Mind clarity and getting to know one's self on a deeper level are brought about by this stone. It attracts positive energy while deflecting negative energy. It is one of the strongest crystals that can shed negative influence in a home. Some types of amethysts are the chevron amethyst and banded amethyst.

Aquamarine: The aquamarine has the ability to equilibrate emotions, boost personal power and clear the mind. Seamen during the ancient times used it to save them from jeopardy in the sea while providing them with bravery. It is related to the heart chakra; thus, helping an individual to promote self-expression and realize the innermost truth.

Aventurine: Aventurine attracts success, abundance, love and luck. It soothes, balances and defends the heart. It is a stone that helps turn one's dreams into reality. Some types of aventurine are red aventurine and peach aventurine.

Azurite: Azurite is also called as "Stone of the Heavens". It helps in pursuing the heavenly self. It awakens psychic capabilities; thus, aiding in the recognition of spiritual guidance and intuition. It soothes and alleviates mental stress, clearing the mind and dissolving blocked energy. Native Americans and Mayans see it as sacred that helps them with mystical communication.

Black Tourmalinated Quartz: Black tourmalinated quartz is a clear quartz with some black tourmaline in it. It is a stone of wealth and great luck. It stimulates enveloping the body with a huge amount of light, which aids in healing. This stone aids in unblocking energy within the body and creating a balance.

Bloodstone: Bloodstone is powerful as a healing crystal. It cleanses the body and in turn, purifies the energy of the body and grounds negative energy. It also boosts strength and energy by providing a constant pouring of energy within the body. This stone is advantageous for athletes.

Blue Lace Agate: Blue lace agate heals and activates the throat chakra. It boosts verbal expression and communication and at the same time raises emotional acceptance. It soothes the nerves, which brings calmness. It is beneficial to people who suffer from depression. One can also use it to alleviate headaches and insomnia.

Carnelian: Carnelian is a belly chakra stone. It raises physical energy and personal power bringing compassion, courage and creativity. It boosts will and vitality; thus, providing the confidence needed in the pursuit of dreams. It is beneficial to use during job interviews as it awakens hidden skills and talents. Ancient Egyptians use carnelian when they bury their loved ones as it was believed that it can defend during the travels to the afterlife and it can soothe anxiety about rebirth.

Chrysocolla: Chrysocolla calms and soothes stress. It is related to the throat chakra, aiding in expressing one's self. It pours out negative energies especially in trying times e.g. job loss. It aids in facing changes and challenges. It also inspires self-awareness and inner balance and raises the capability to love.

Chrysoprase: Chrysoprase activates and opens the heart chakra. It permits a great energy flow to the heart. Infusion with universal love results to giving divine energies. It is a stone of compassion and grace; thus, promoting contentment, joy, and optimism and enhancing self-acceptance.

Citrine: Citrine is a crystal of happiness and light. It does not keep negative energy; thus, cleansing is not necessary. It gives clarity and activates the imagination. As it is controlled by the sun, it energizes and cleanses the body, specifically the solar plexus.

Clear Quartz: The clear quartz activates and energizes energy centers contained in the body. It gives clarity bringing focus to clear dreams and desires. It also helps in removing energy blockages within the body.

Coral: Coral is also referred to as "garden of the sea". It prevents bad fortune and protects against skin disease. Dreaming about corals predicts recovery from an illness. It aids in visualization and meditation because it represents blood-force energy and life.

Freshwater Pearl: Freshwater pearl is grown in inland waters. It brings beauty, love and light. It enhances awareness and consciousness of problems. It is related with innocence and aids in seeing life with compassion.

Garnet: Garnet boosts pleasure, passion, and energy. It is believed that the sole light in Noah's ark was given by a garnet crystal. It aids in moving the energy flow and chi in the body; thus, encouraging physical activity. It also aids with depression because it brings hope and joy and reduces anger. It purifies negative energy chakras while invigorating them. Some types of garnet are green garnet and hessonite garnet.

Goldstone: Goldstone is produced from quartz sand glass and inoculated with copper particles that give it a shiny appearance. It symbolizes light and can easily be located in the darkness. It diverts negative energy and is a protective stone.

Hematite: Hematite protects and lets one stay grounded in a situation. It takes in negative energy and soothes stress. When worn, a balanced, centered, and calm emotion is felt. It aids in finding talents and releases limitations.

Jade: Jade attracts luck. It helps in attaining dreams and goals and allows you to see past limitations. It enhances compassion, courage, longevity, and generosity, thereby helping in leading a fulfilling life.

Jasper: Jasper is bursting with grounding energy. It can enjoin an individual with the Earth's vibrations; therefore, giving an in-depth understanding of nature's power. It also aids us in critical thinking. It is sacred for some Native Americans as it symbolizes the Earth's blood. Some types of jasper are the black jasper, exotica jasper, rainforest jasper, Dalmatian jasper, fancy jasper, king cobra jasper, kambaba jasper, leopard skin jasper, ocean jasper, poppy jasper, succor creek jasper, mookaite jasper, red jasper, yellow jasper, picture jasper, and zebra jasper.

Labradorite: Labradorite opens and purifies the crown chakra by encouraging the owner's intuition. It allows you to see reality and identify goals and dreams. You can use it to enhance imagination, see clearly during meditation, and unfold passion.

Lapis Lazuli: Lapis lazuli had lived since ancient times. It is capable of enjoining the owner to higher truth. It aids in fostering verbal expression and opening and equilibrating the throat chakra. It gives wisdom and links an individual with his spiritual guide, which protects from negative energy and makes the negative vibrations return to their origin.

Malachite: Malachite aids in purifying and clearing all chakras. It equilibrates and stimulates the throat and heart chakras, making it an overall healing stone. It releases negative experiences, making an individual regain hope. It is compassionate, purifying and inspiring. It is able to attract love by unfolding the heart.

Moonstone: Moonstone is the destiny stone. It has a strong relationship to the divine feminine and to the moon; thus, it is beneficial to women. It raises fertility and balances the mind. It aids in aligning the production of hormones, reproduction, and metabolism and allows in-depth emotions to surface. One type of moonstone is the rainbow moonstone.

Mother of Pearl: Mother of pearl is the lining that is developed in mollusks. It is related to water and the ocean, making it contain a strong healing energy. It is considered to deflect evil and reduces fear, and further good luck and prosperity; therefore, permitting an individual to see beauty in simple things.

Obsidian: Obsidian is developed from lava that has undergone cooling quickly. It enjoins the root chakra to the Earth's core. It cleanses and sheds negative energy and aids in releasing negative emotions e.g. fear, anger, greed, and jealousy. Some types of obsidian are mahogany obsidian, rainbow obsidian, and snowflake obsidian.

Onyx: Onyx protects the body and mind against electromagnetic energy. It takes in and converts negative energy while preventing the drainage of personal energy. It aids in releasing depression and negativity and in calming fears; therefore, leaving an individual with a secure and stable feeling.

Peridot: Peridot has been used as a healing crystal for several millennia. It is carrying positive energy, which is beneficial to those experiencing distress. It is Archangel Rafael's stone and dominates the Angelic virtues' realm. It is able to bring out light, happiness, and unconditional love.

Pyrite: Pyrite has the ability to mend financial hardships and attracting abundance. It symbolizes good luck and money due to its resemblance to gold. Because of its golden color, it is associated with the sun and with boosting the mind. It is an amazing energy shield as it blocks out negative energies.

Rhodonite: Rhodonite equilibrates emotions and brings patience. It functions with the heart chakra in order to ground negativity, raise awareness on parts of life that needs improvements, and attract love. It aids in discovering inner talents and brings out love. It also helps in finding out true passion.

Rhodochrosite: Rhodochrosite increases self-worth and self-esteem while raising self-love. It stimulates loving one's self and achieving a state of happiness; thus, it is mainly used for emotional healing. It is a wonderful heart chakra crystal, which vibrates with love energy. It also provides the bravery to face challenges.

Rose Quartz: The rose quartz is the crystal for unconditional love. It opens the heart to different types of love such as familial love, friendship, romantic love, and self-love. It nurtures forgiveness, reconciliation and empathy. It also reduces stress and heart tensions. It can release jealousy, resentment, and anger, which eventually leads to heart healing.

Rudraksha Seeds: Rudraksha seeds give out positive vibrations. They contain a large amount of cosmic powers that help in elevating the soul and aiding on the path of greatness. Based on ancient Vedas, these seeds are the tears shed by Shiva to help heal humanity.

Rutilated Quartz: The rutilated quartz is the clear quartz infused with golden rutile. It can unblock energy of all chakras and align the body and mind. It is capable of attuning to the divine purpose. It is an uplifting stone that is able to infuse joy into one's life and environment. It hastens the mending of injuries and slows down aging effects.

Selenite: Selenite is mainly used for energy clearing. It can protect and clear an individual's energy body and clear the crystals' energy at the same time. It unblocks negative energy rapidly to develop a great flow of positive energy. It magnifies the energy of near gemstones; thus, recharging them. Recently, it has been used in holistic medical treatments such as tumor reduction and cancer treatment.

Serpentine: Serpentine brings hormonal balance. It aids in releasing crowded chakra areas making healing possible. It raises awareness of self-responsibility. It is a reminder of the possibility of achieving goals. It also attracts an individual's wants in life.

Smoky Quartz: Smoky quartz aids in grounding and connecting to the Earth. It gives off a high amount of energy that takes in and transforms negative energy. It aids in shedding emotional and mental blockages; thus, alleviating pain and deflecting negative energy. It is mainly used for dissolving resentment and anger and emotional support.

Sodalite: Sodalite fosters self-truth and self-expression. It aids in dealing with problems regarding self-esteem, self-acceptance and self-worth. It enhances intuition and self-trust and awakens the third eye, making meditating go deeper.

Sunstone: Sunstone has a strong connection to light and the sun. It provides light to any situation and a positive attitude. It contains a bright energy, which raises vitality and uplifts mood. It also empowers those who are suffering from abandonment and motivates positive outlook.

Tiger's Eye: Tiger's eye equilibrates all levels of the body. It encourages an optimistic outlook towards the future and provides light in all situations and insight in all challenges. It also attracts good luck, prosperity, and abundance to the owner. It was used as an amulet during ancient civilizations to defend against curses and bad luck. Some types of tiger's eye are American tiger's eye, red tiger's eye and blue tiger's eye.

Turquoise: Turquoise is also referred to as the master healer. It is believed to be connecting the heaven, earth and sky. Many cultures of Native America believe that it bridges the mind to the universe's immeasurable possibilities and it is seen as sacred by the Chinese. Being a throat chakra, it promotes honest communication. It also functions to align and protect chakras while strengthening the body.

Purchasing crystals is easy, however, they are never owned truly. Losing a crystal often represents that it has discovered a new home where its power is more useful. A strong urge to pass it on may also be felt, which represents the same thing. Healing crystals are excellent in giving out intuitive messages when they want to be given away.

Because some crystals contain strong energy, it can be overpowering when carried or worn on a day to day basis. These kinds of crystals are the ones often lost because being stimulated by very powerful energies is not advantageous. However, when they are needed, they resurface or you may replace them with a more appropriate crystal; thus, looking for them is not necessary. It is best to permit crystals to approach and leave because they accomplish their best work when restrictions are not present.

Chapter 4 - Clearing Crystals

Clearing is the process of cleansing healing crystals. It should be done after purchasing, before healing, and after every healing. A clear crystal gives better effects than an unclear crystal. It also feels bright and positive, cold and tingly when touched. On the other hand, an unclear crystal may feel drained, heavy, or hot. The following are ways to clear crystals effectively and efficiently.

Sea Salt Method: The sea salt method is done by burying the crystal in sea salt overnight. It is preferred that the crystal be contained in a glass or ceramic container. Intuition is used to identify the length of time the crystal should be cleared. However, it is usually done for one to three days then washed them with water.

Smudging: A burning sage or cedar is used to smudge the crystals. It is a good way to ensure that the crystals are purified. It is done by holding the burning cedar or sage while passing the stone in the smoke.

Moonlight: Clearing by means of moonlight is done by placing the crystals outside during the full moon to new moon. It clears crystals by dispelling old energies. The length of time is different with every healer as it depends on his sensitivity. It is recommended to hang the crystals in a tree where the moonlight can shine on them.

Burying: Burying crystals into the earth is done when deep clearing is required. The length of time is dependent on the owner. Burying with herbs can also be done. Sage, rose petals, sandalwood and myrrh are used and it is a delicate way to clear them. However, it takes longer.

The Sacred Breath: The sacred breath is done by blowing on the crystal while asking an individual's higher self to clear it. It blows away any negative energy contained in the crystal.

Cool Tap Water: You can also use clear tap water to clear the crystals. You can do this by running the crystal under the water. It is necessary that the points face down the sink to ensure that any negativity will go down. Warm or hot water should not be used as it will break the crystal.

Chapter 5 - Dedicating and Programming Crystals

After selecting and clearing a crystal, programming it is also beneficial. It is done to concentrate its benefits to something that the individual truly needs; therefore, intensifying the crystal's intent to the individual. Dedicating a crystal to a God or Goddess is to defend it against negativity. A dedicated and programmed crystal makes it more useful and powerful.

Programming is a simple process. It is done by holding the crystal and sensing its energy. When the crystal is newly cleared, a stronger energy is felt, which is more appealing. When the energy is sensed and appreciated, quietly ask to be linked to the crystal's deva. Even though crystals are inanimate objects, they are alive and the crystal's life-force energy is referred to as the deva.

Once sensed, ponder on what it is going to be used for. Ponder on this and then ask the crystal quietly if it agrees. The energy of the crystal will increase if it agrees and will decrease if it does not. Once programmed, its intent will not change unless someone reprograms it.

Dedicating, on the other hand, is done by simply holding the crystal and clearly stating with your mind the words, "Only the most positive high-level energy may work through this healing tool". Emphasize on this and then end it by saying "So be it". Through this, dedication takes place.

One may also dedicate the crystal to a healing energy e.g. the healing goddess. Some healing goddesses are the White Buffalo Calf Woman, Yemaya, Isis, and Diana. For crystals that are programmed for defense, Kali and Hecate are powerful protection goddesses.

Chapter 6 - How to Use Crystals

Crystals can be used in various ways. It just depends on the preference of the owner. The most common ways to use crystals are mentioned as follows.

Worn on the body or close to the body: Individuals who have no knowledge regarding crystal healing will most often choose healing crystals by intuition. Crystals that are worn or kept close to the body are usually used for protection and healing. They affect the energy field and the body. The location of the crystal will not affect its power in most cases. However, placing it on or adjacent to the specific area that needs treatment will result to faster recovery as it gives an emphasized effect. The healing energy will focus on the area where healing is most needed. The energy can also be directed by intent. A crystal can also be put in little pouches and then be pinned to clothing.

The greatest effect of the crystal when worn as a pendant will depend on the length of the chain. When resting at the throat chakra, it will have stronger results on areas that are dominated by the throat chakra such as creativity and communication. Even if that is the case, it will still give energy to the entire physical body. On the other hand, when it is worn near the heart, it will affect the heart chakra more than any other chakra.

Kept under a pillow: Keeping a crystal under a pillow can aid in sleeping problems such as insomnia. Some crystals can protect against psychic attacks and nightmares. Others can help in recalling dreams while some can aid in astral travel and out of body experiences.

Used in the bath: A crystal can be submerged in bathwater or placed at the edge of the tub. This is helpful in cleansing the body on all levels. It can shed off strain and stress; thus, invigorating an individual. Putting a crystal in the bath will take in negative emotions and energy. One effective crystal to use in the bath is adventurine. Rose quartz, amethyst, and clear quartz can be used, too.

In meditation practice: A crystal's energy structure provides order and stillness to the body, which aids in calming the mind. Changing the way of thinking will help in finding solutions. A crystal can be positioned in front of the individual during meditation or it can be held.

Placed around the home or workplace: Placing a crystal around the home or workplace is usually done for room cleansing and space clearing. A crystal is capable of altering a space's energy; thus, lightening up the atmosphere and cancelling out negativity. It can also add balance to a space. Intuition is used in determining where to place a crystal. Crystal clusters and raw crystals retain energy integrity better than single crystals. With this, they are able to absorb more negativity before needing cleansing.

Counteracting environmental pollution: Being subjected every day to harmful substances such as electricity, plastics, microwaves and radio waves, an individual's body usually suffers from environmental stress. The mentioned substances raise stress loading resulting to increased susceptibility to diseases. These substances can reduce the geomagnetic field, the earth's natural electromagnetic field, by giving off greater electromagnetic resonances which hinder natural frequencies.

Electrical devices create strong electromagnetic field around themselves causing entrainment. Entrainment occurs when the body's natural frequencies and a greater outside force's frequencies are enjoined. One can use crystals to increase personal energy fields that can cancel out environmental stress' effects.

Making gem essences: A gem essence is the type of the energy patterns of a crystal in liquid form. It is produced with water that has unique characteristics, making a gem essence effective. Being in liquid form, it can be used in ways that a crystal cannot. Proper measures should be practiced when making a gem essence because crystals can be toxic. A gem essence is done by putting a crystal in a bowl with enough spring water to cover it. The bowl containing the crystal and water is then placed in under sunlight for two hours.

A storage bottle is then half-filled with brandy and then filled to the top with gem essence. Gem water is made by putting a crystal in a bowl containing spring water and then left overnight. Gem water and gem essence can be consumed during daytime. You can also use them when bathing and as a spray. Because the gem essence is very potent, diluting the gem essence is necessary before using it.

Aura cleansing: Aura cleansing is done by using a clear quartz wand or point to brush the aura several times flicking it away from the body. This clears any negativity, which may be causing ailments.

Laying on of stones. The laying on of stones is done to let go of emotional, etheric, spiritual, and mental blockages. The role of the healer is to bring comfort and support and not be judgmental. This provides the patient with security when releasing emotions. This is done by placing varying crystals on each chakra. This tones and empowers the entire system. Crystals on the lowest chakra are placed first then preceded by an upward move. Placing a grounding crystal such as smoky quartz between feet can be beneficial as it acts as an anchor. When removing the crystals, the highest one is taken first.

Conclusion

Thank you again for downloading the book, *"Crystals: The Complete Crystal Healing Guide (Heal the Body, Mind, and Soul with these Amazing Crystals)"*.

You have now gained knowledge on all the necessary information about crystal healing. You have learned how it works, how you can use it, and most importantly its many benefits. You have found out how to select the right crystals for you and also how to clear, program, and dedicate them.

I hope this book was able to help you discover and understand crystal healing and its many effects on the human body such as relieving stress, alleviating pain, and calming the mind.

What are you waiting for?

Go to the nearest supplier of crystals and try them yourself or visit the nearest New Age clinic. It is also advantageous if you can share this to your friends and do crystal healing together.

Balance your chakras!

Thank you, good luck and spread the word!

Finally, if you enjoyed this book, then I'd like to ask you for a favor, would you be kind enough to leave a review for this book on Amazon? It'd be greatly appreciated!

Printed in Great Britain
by Amazon